BOTANICAL DESIGNS
ADULT COLORING BOOK IV
- An Adult Coloring Book -

What makes our books unique & different from all the others?

We're the only adult coloring book publisher who uses original antique botanical art in our books. Over the years we've acquired an extensive collection of antique images that we're excited to share with you.

AND

We're the only publisher who can show you images of the original antique art.

Want to refer to the original art for coloration? If you'd like to see the original art before our conversion to black and white, visit the Book Images section of our website at http://www.BotanicalArtDesigns com and click on the cover image of the book. You'll be presented with a PDF of the original color images (in as found condition) to use as references as you color.

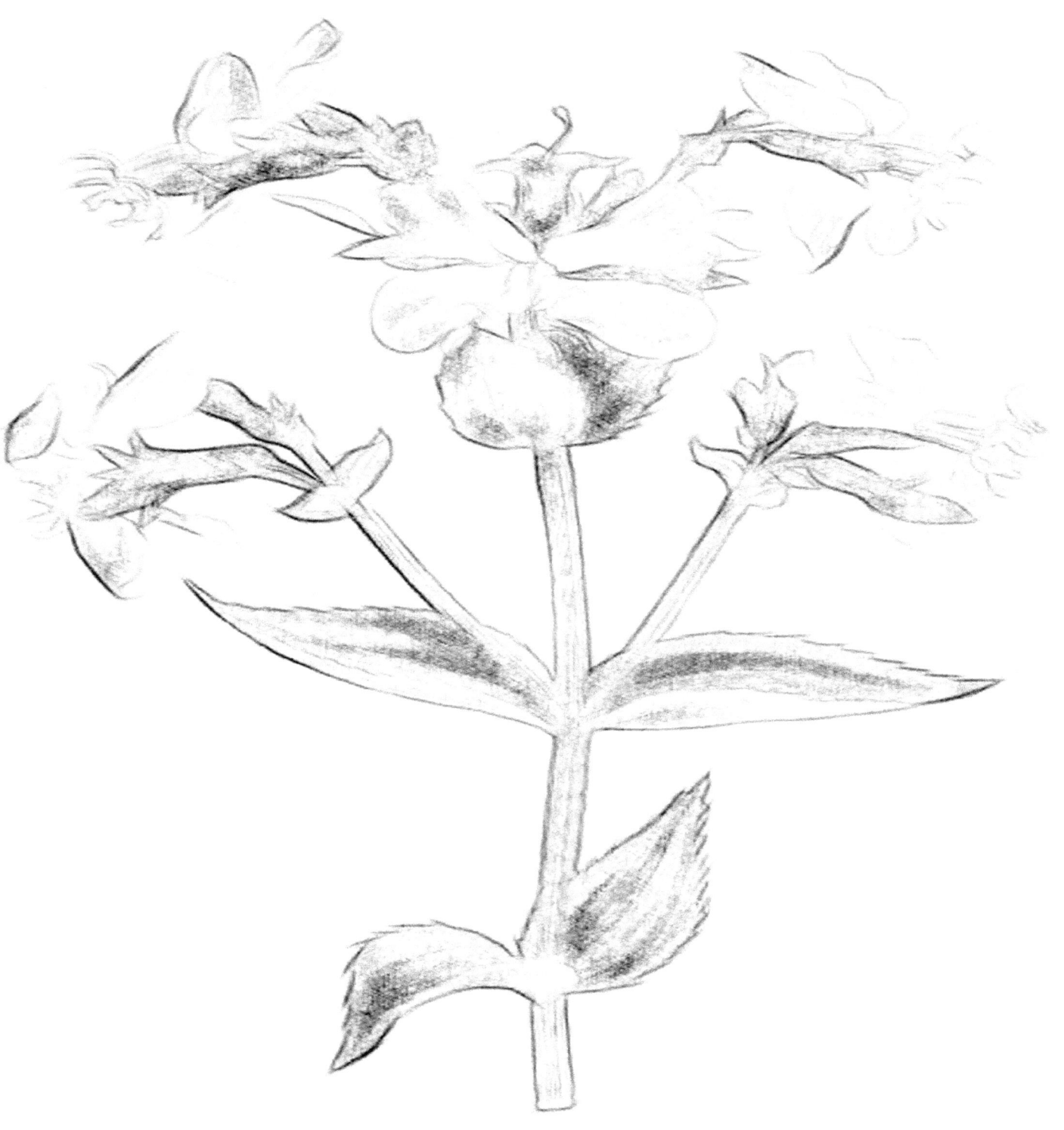

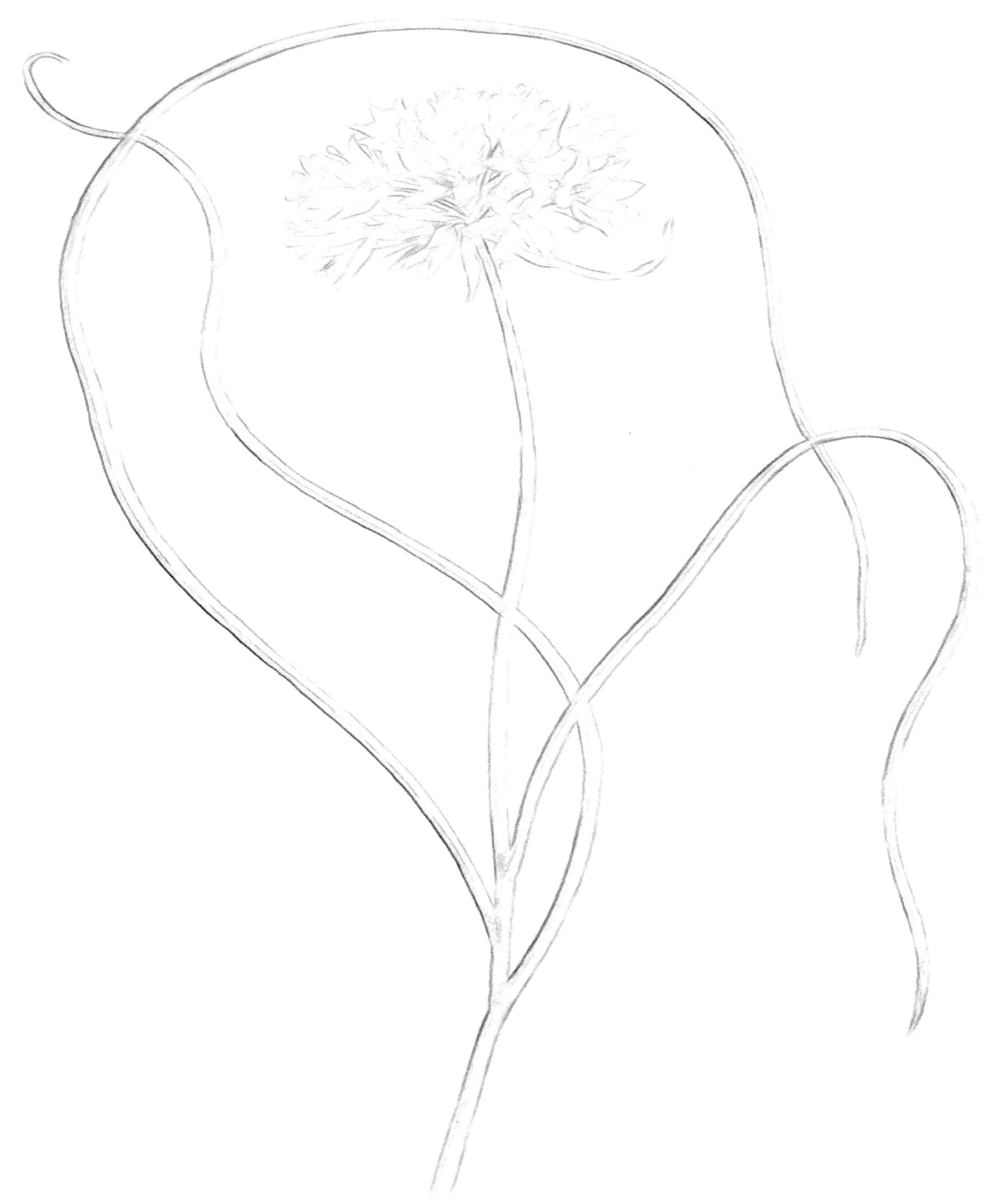

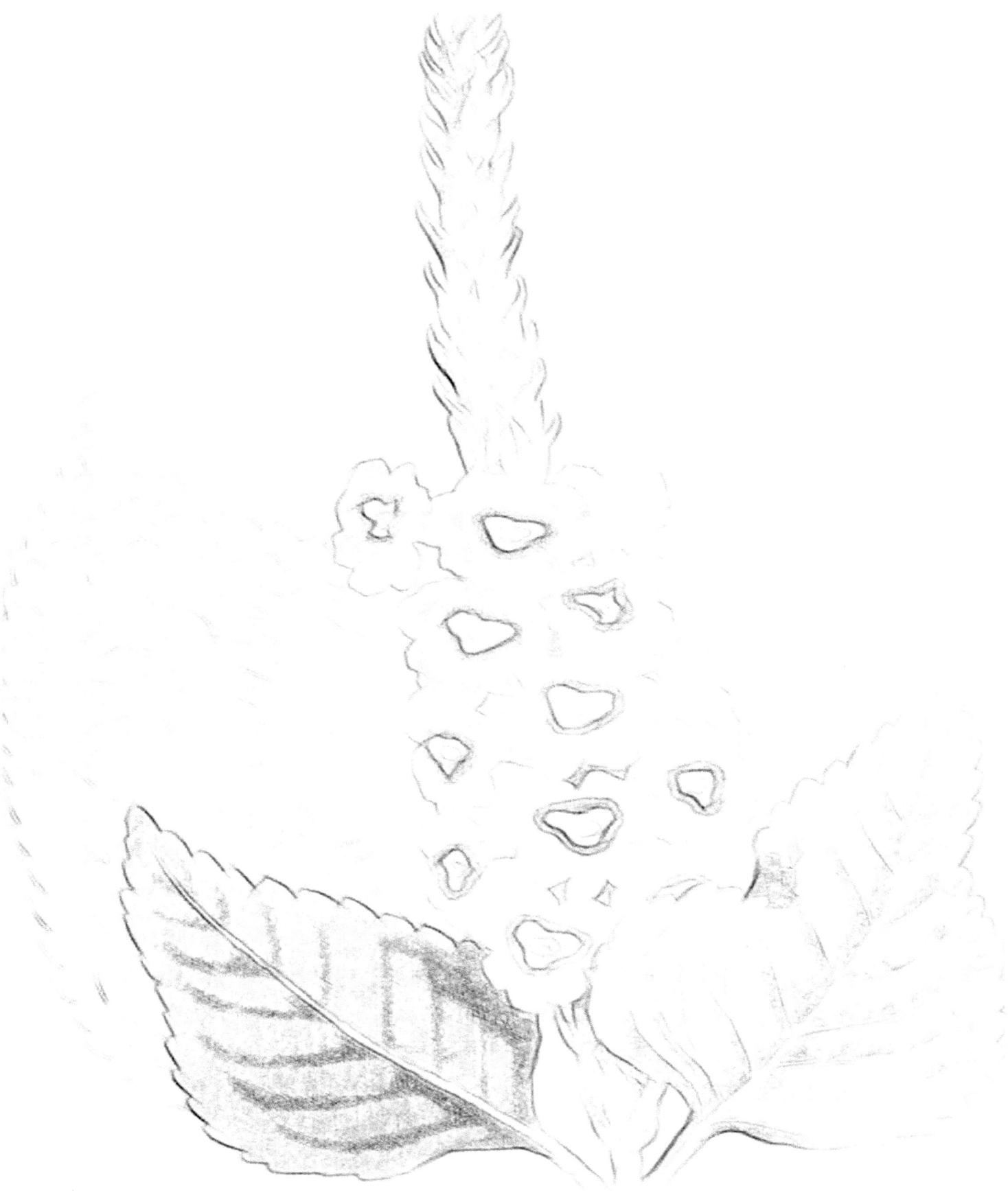

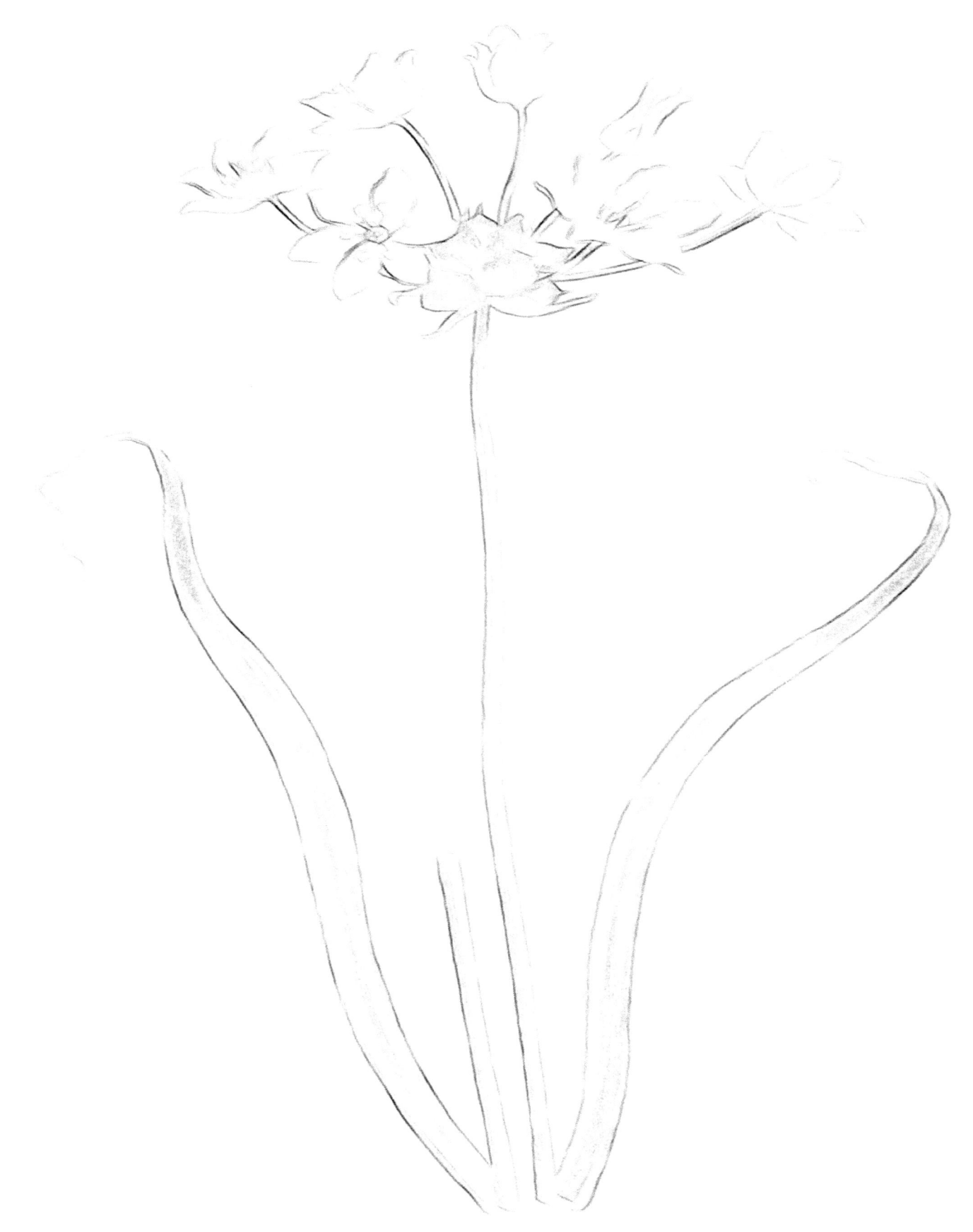

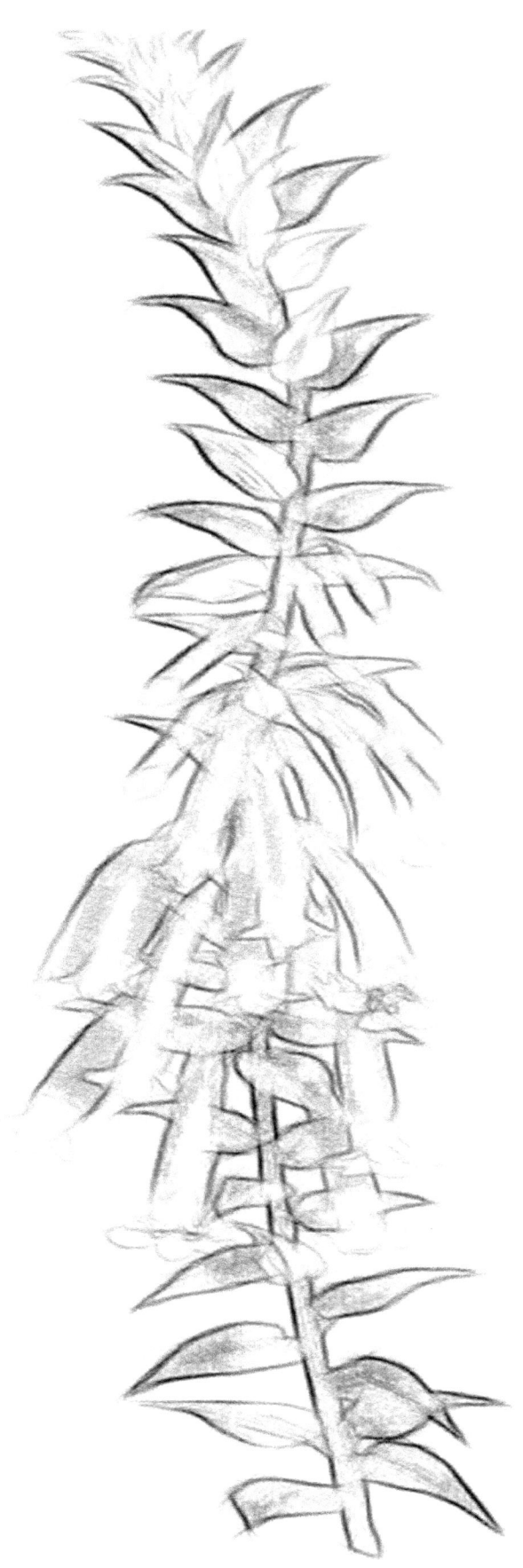

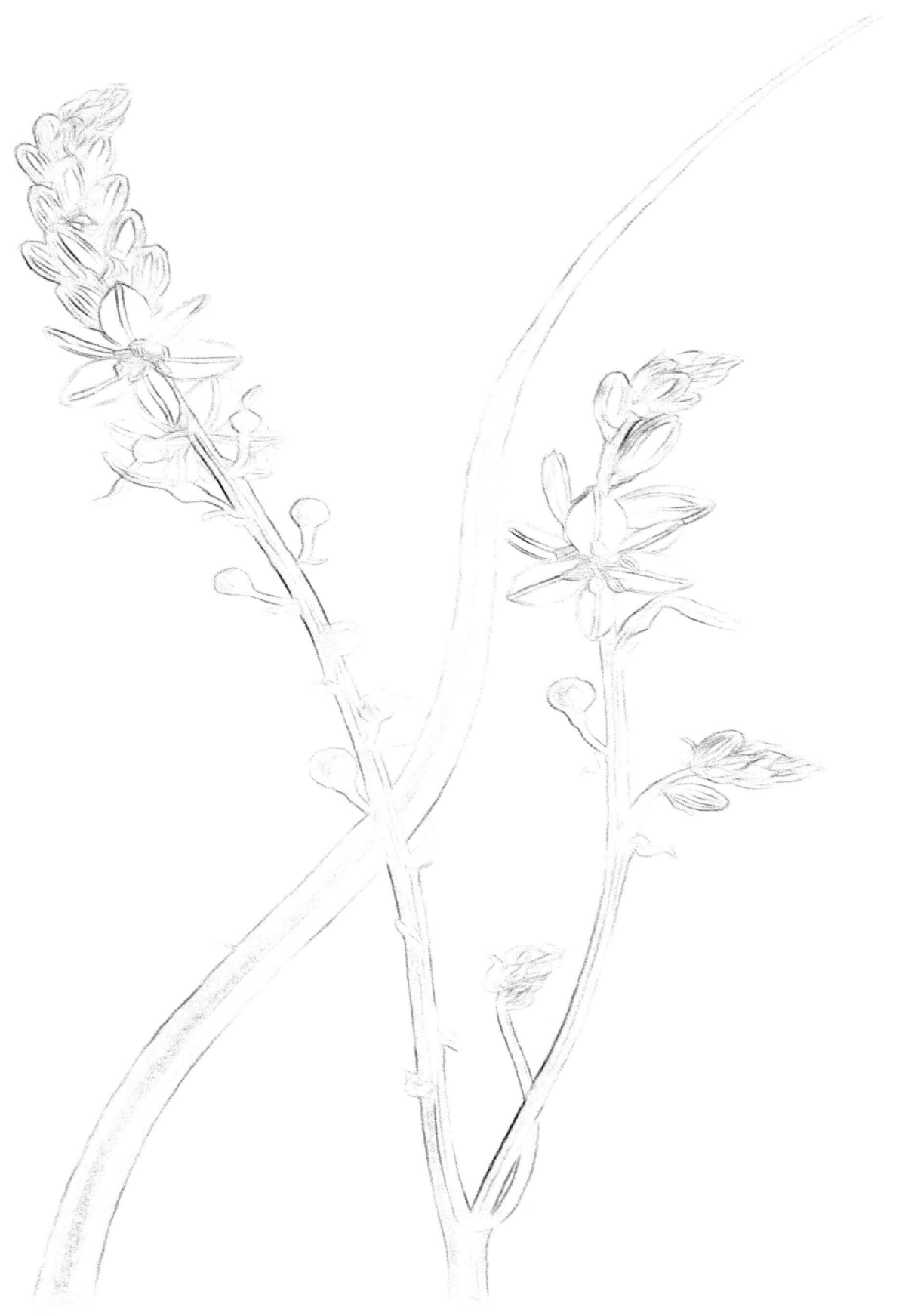

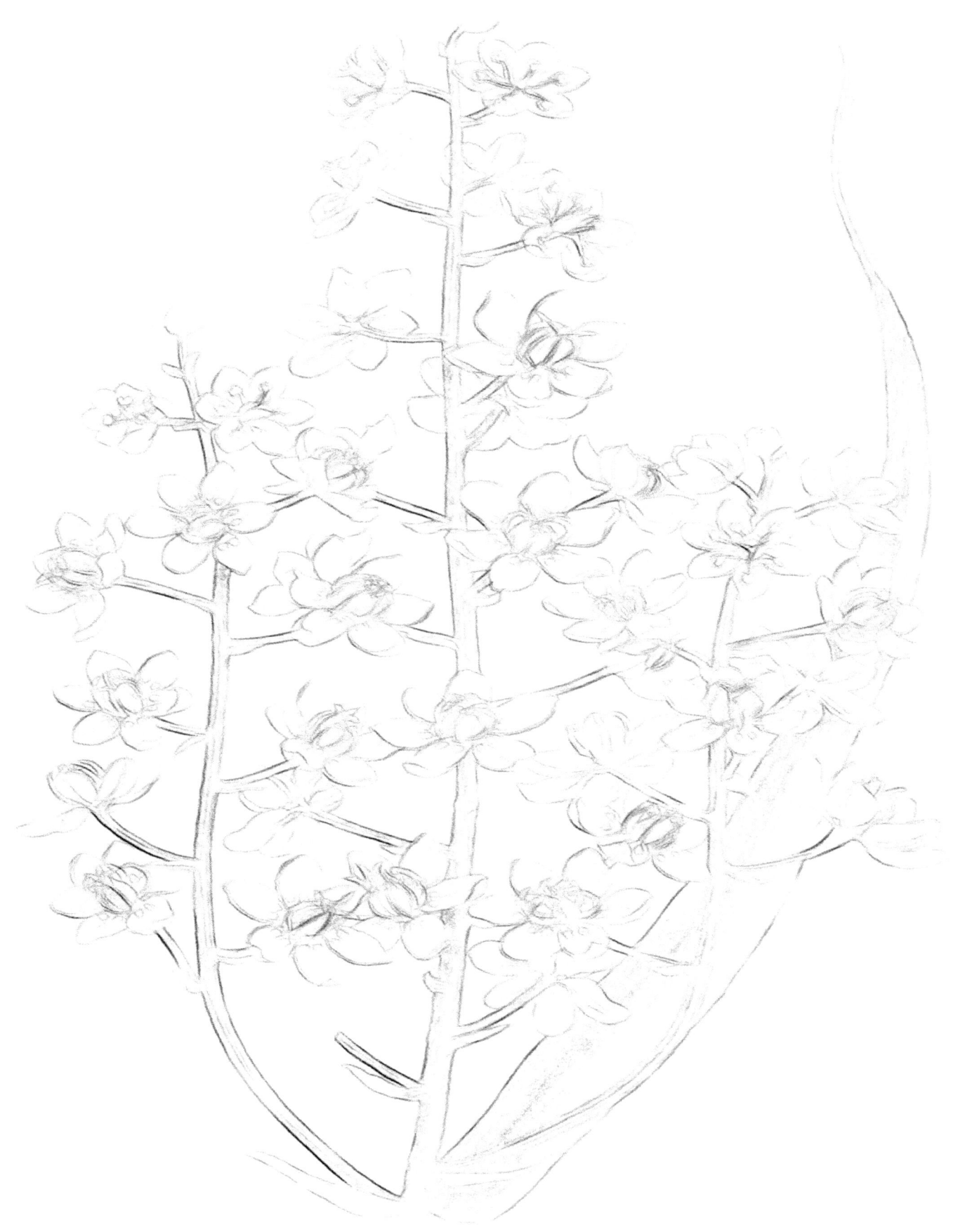

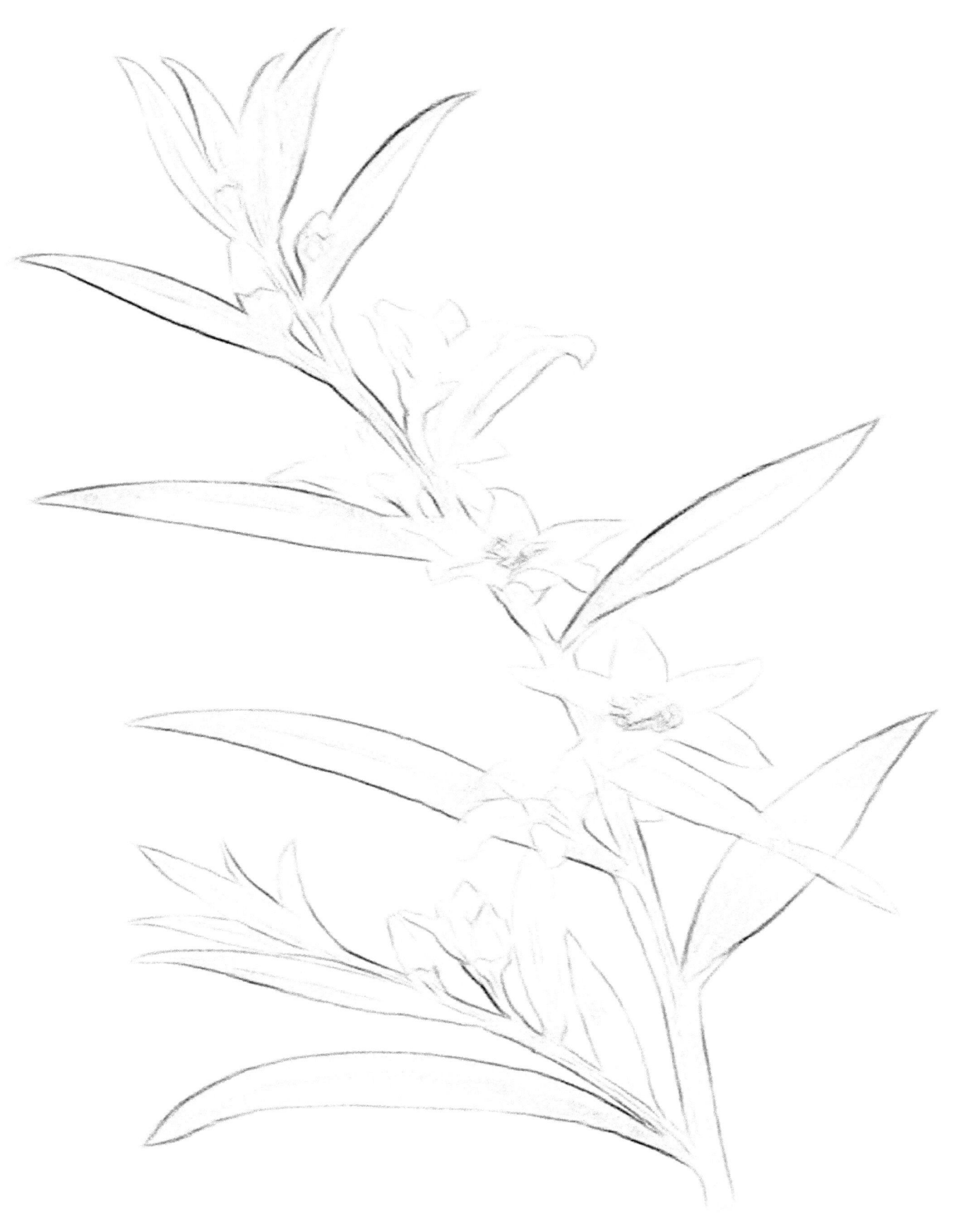

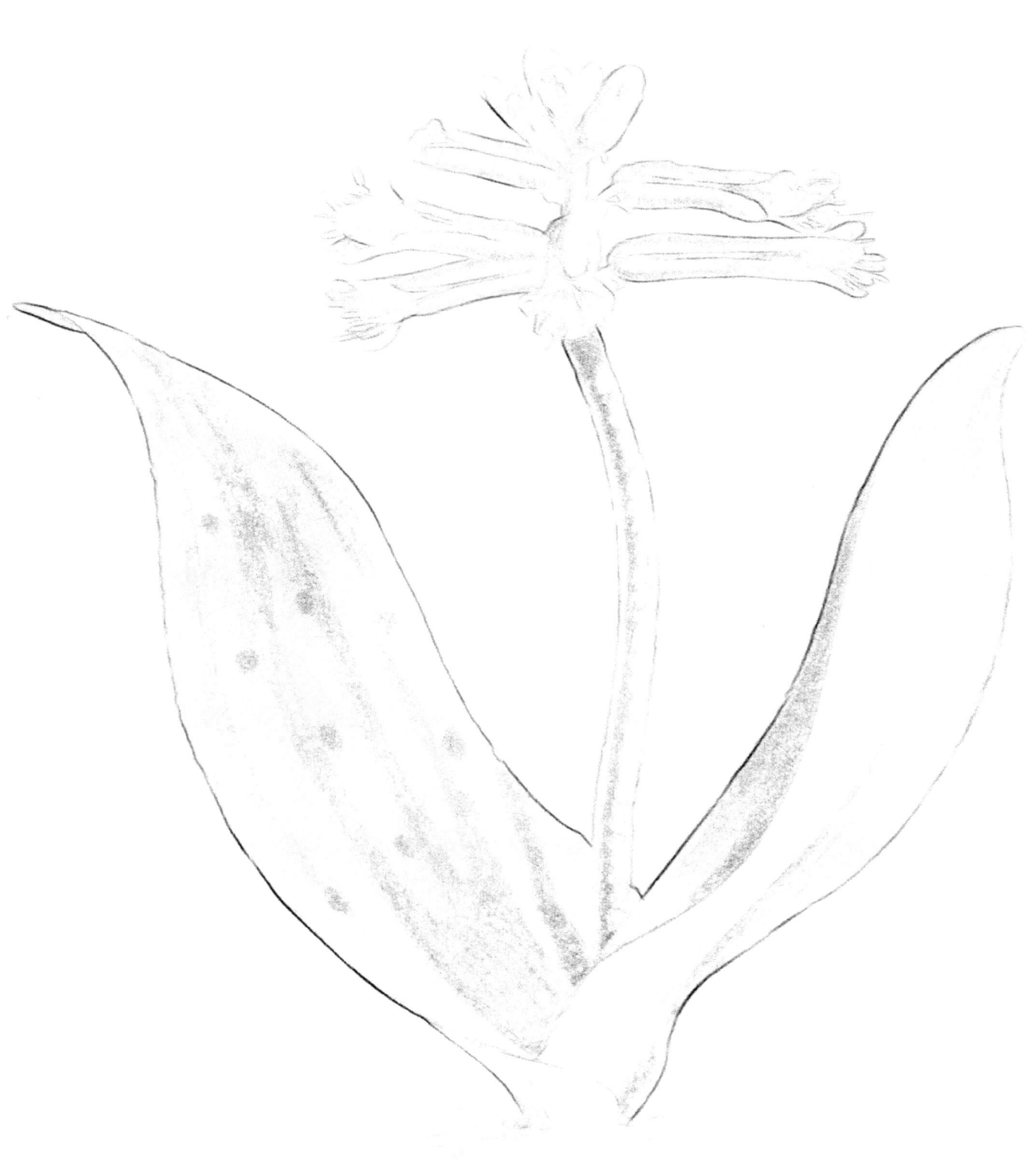

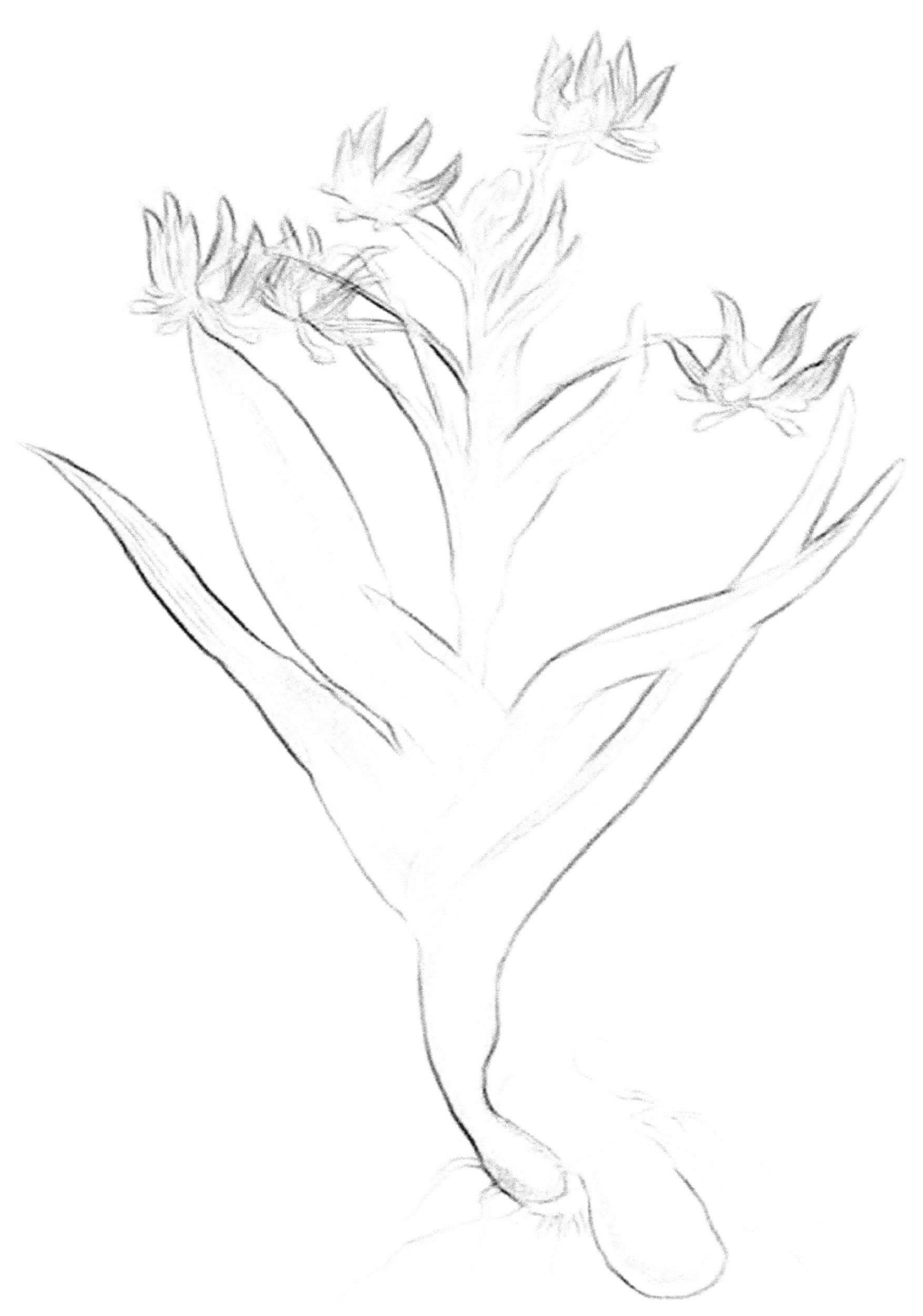

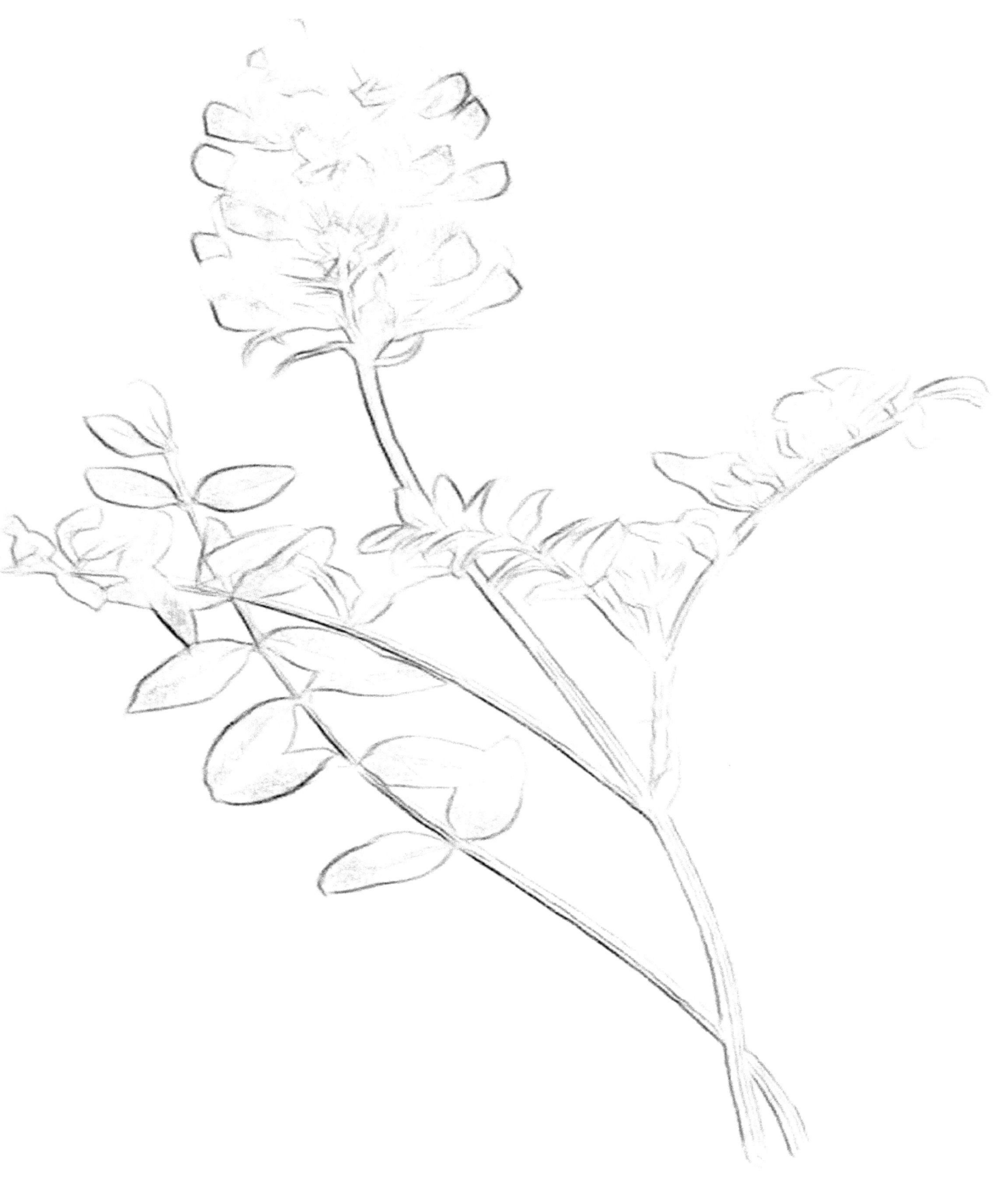

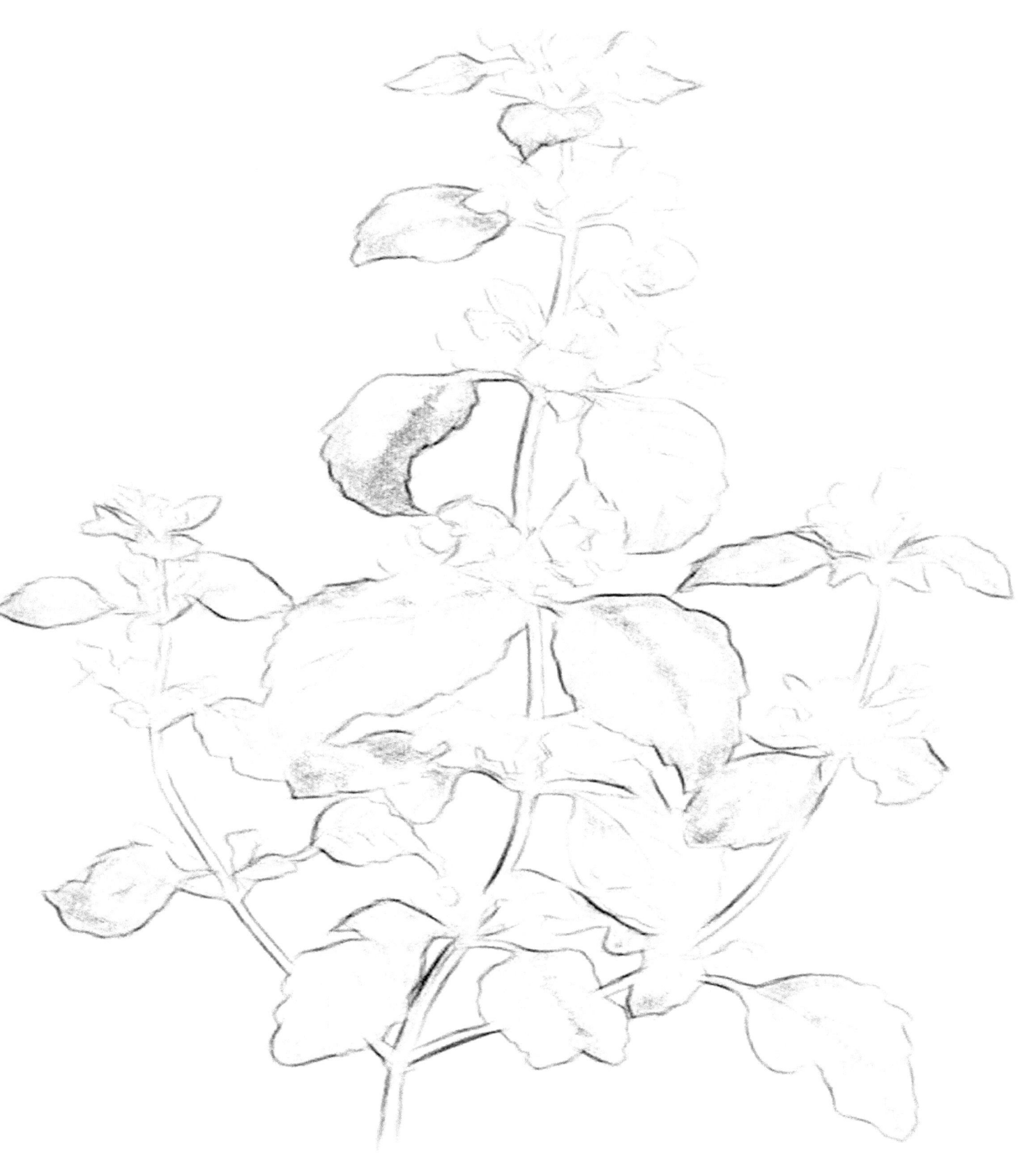

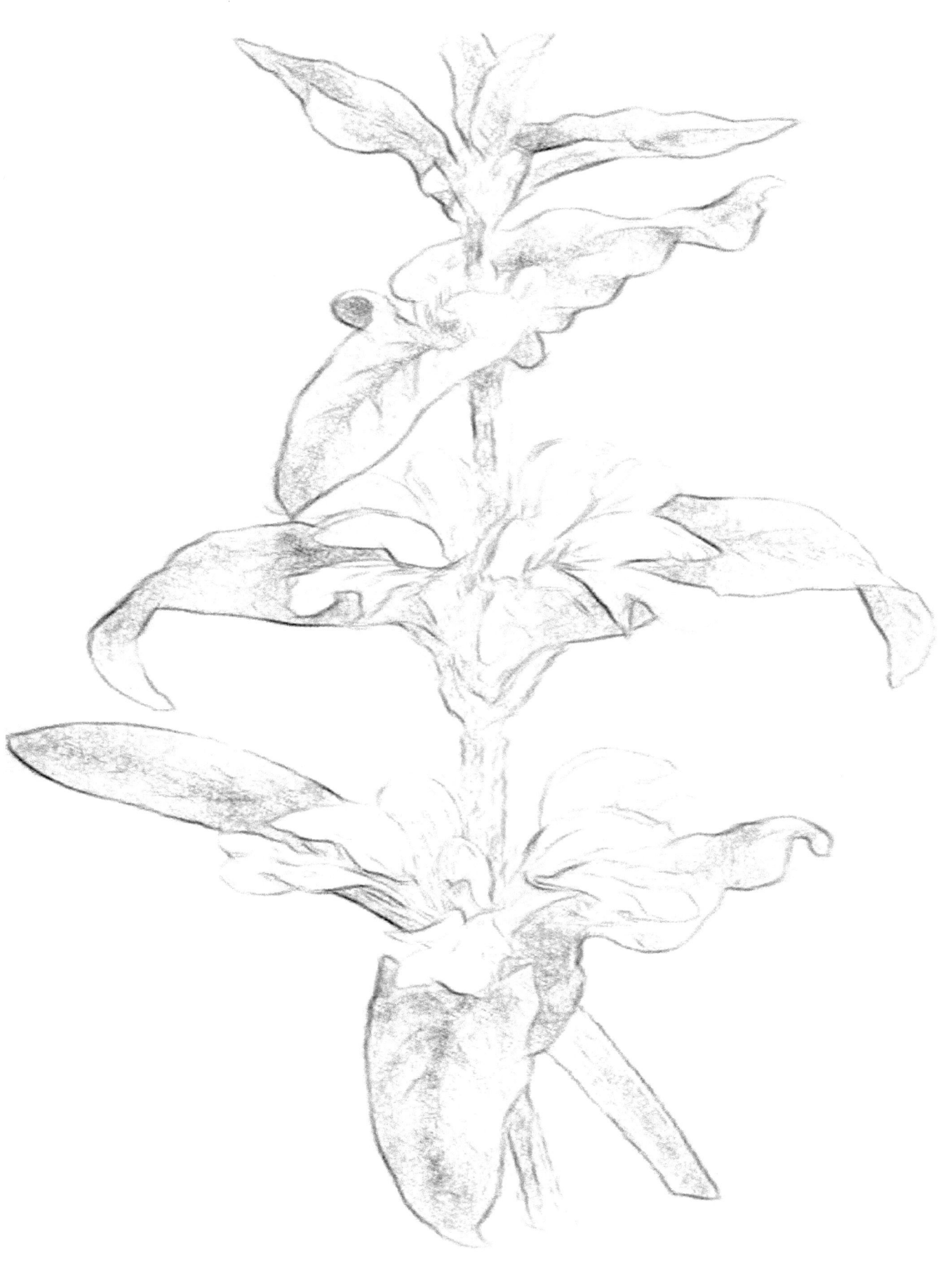

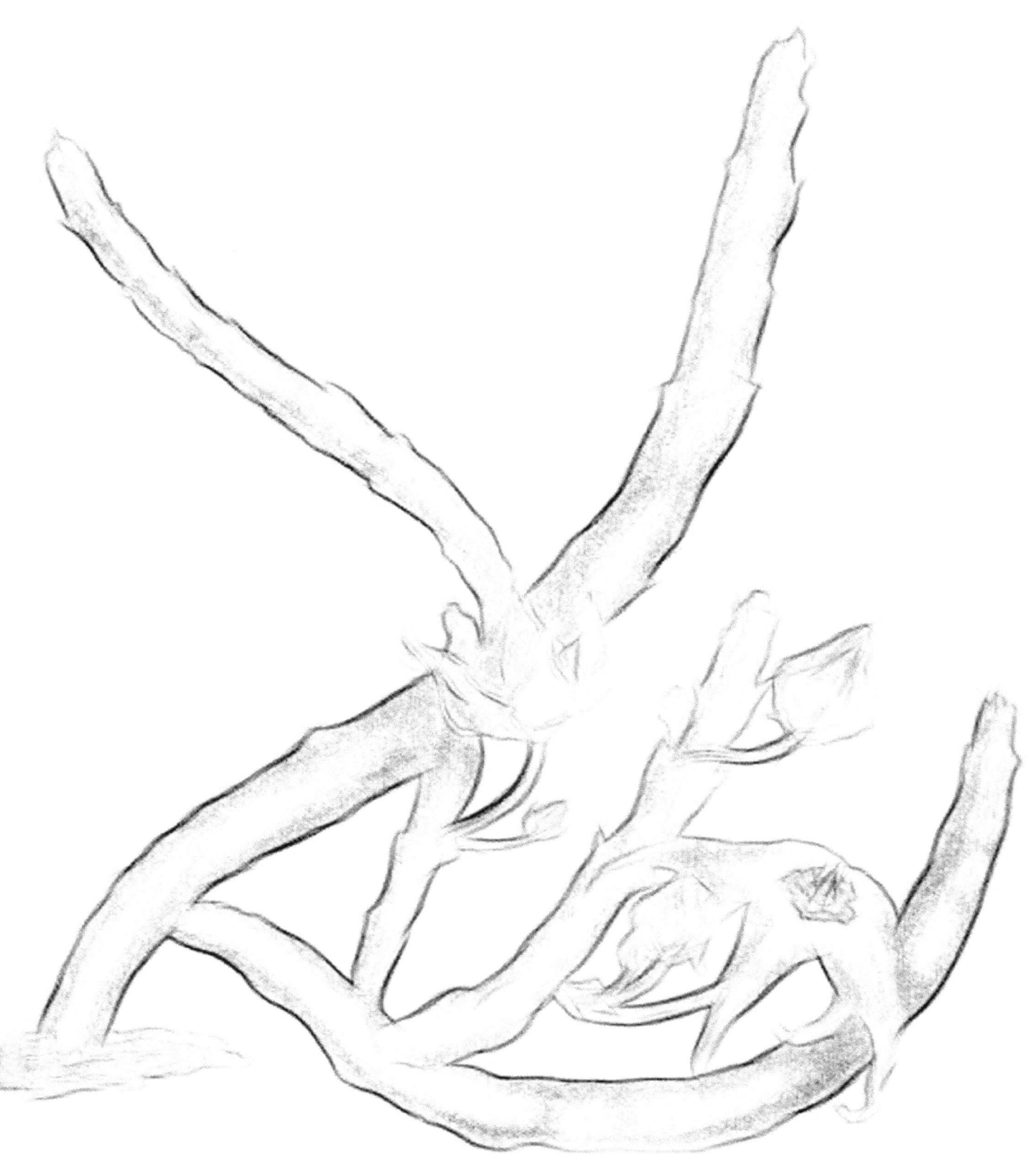

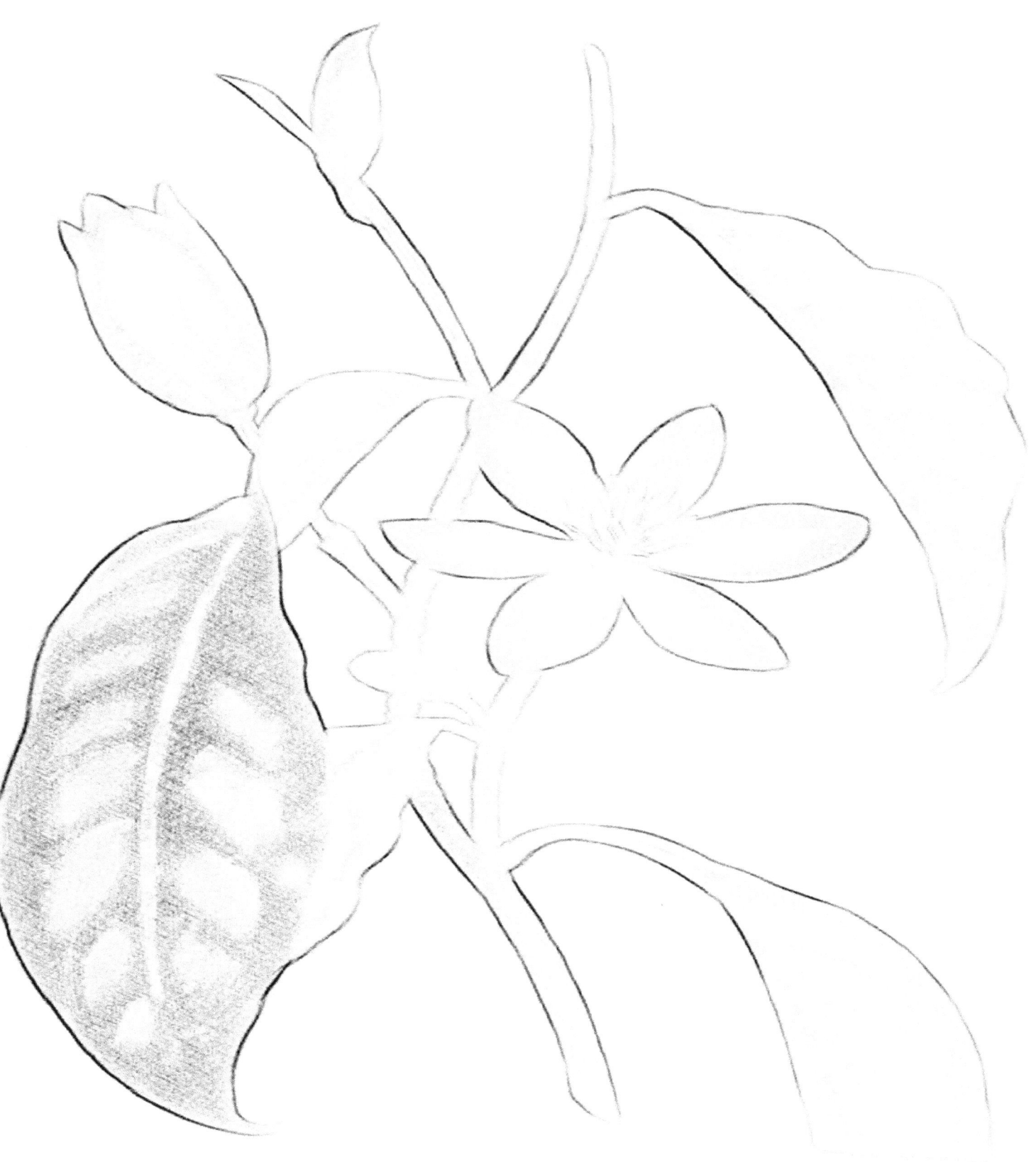

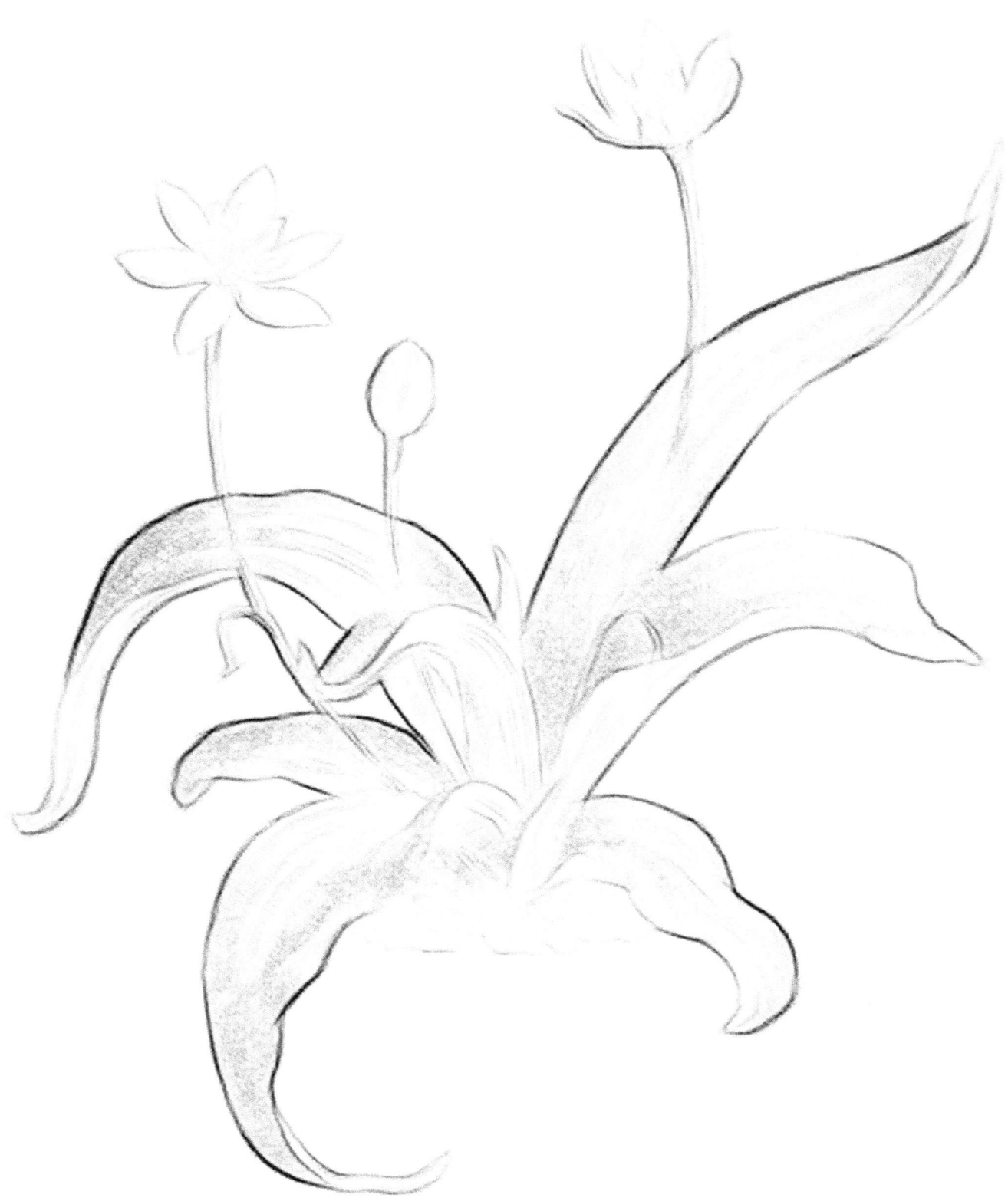

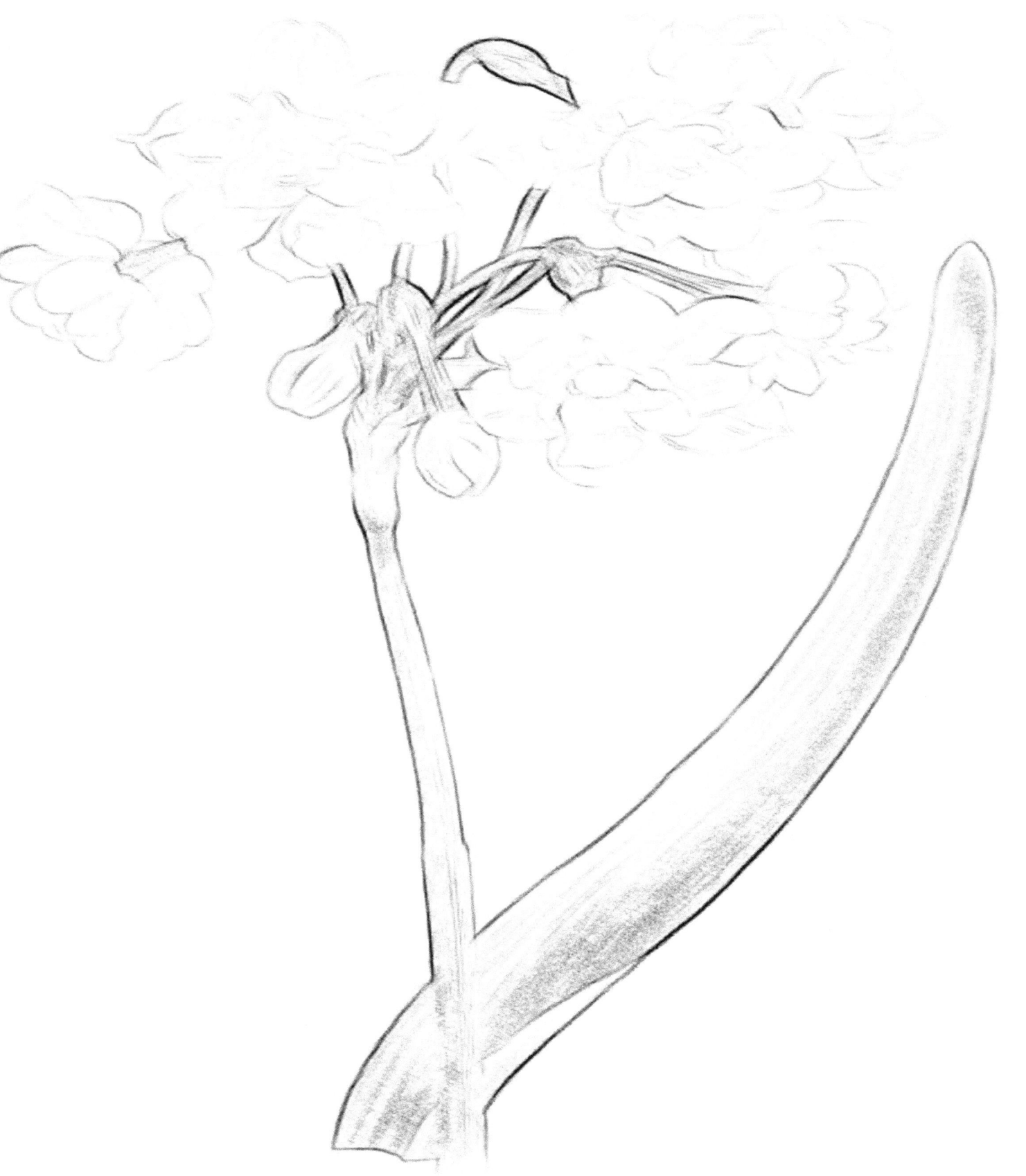

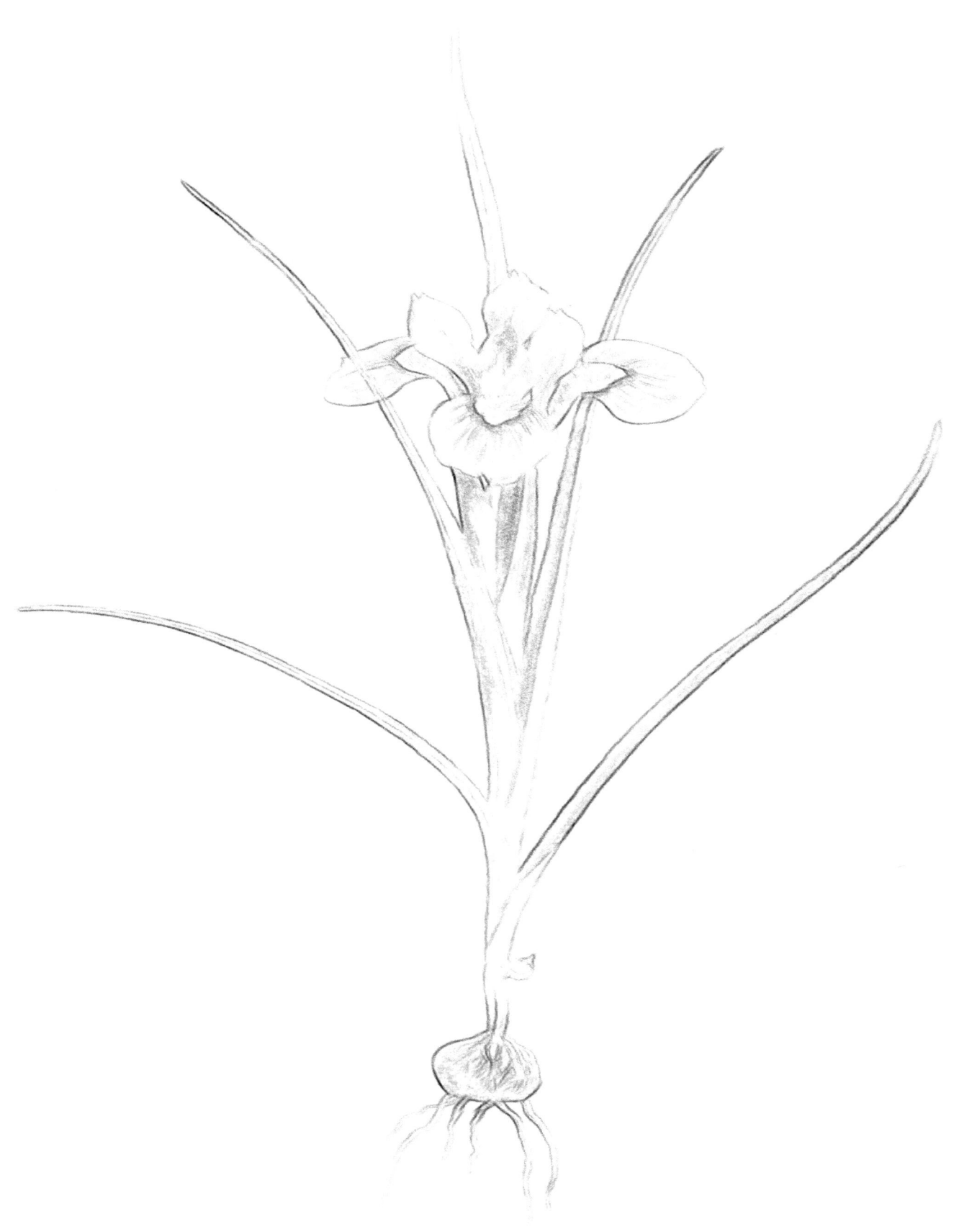

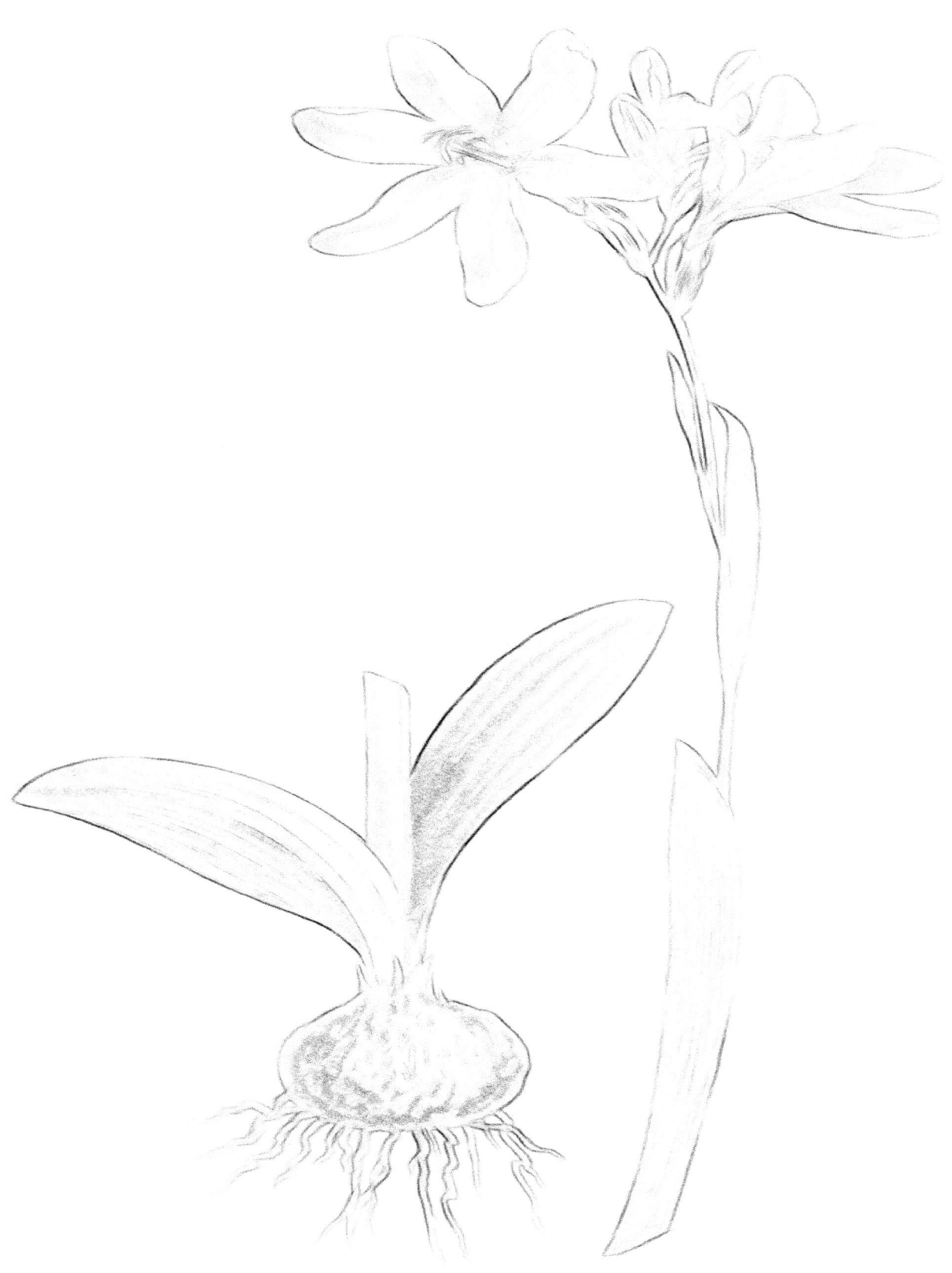

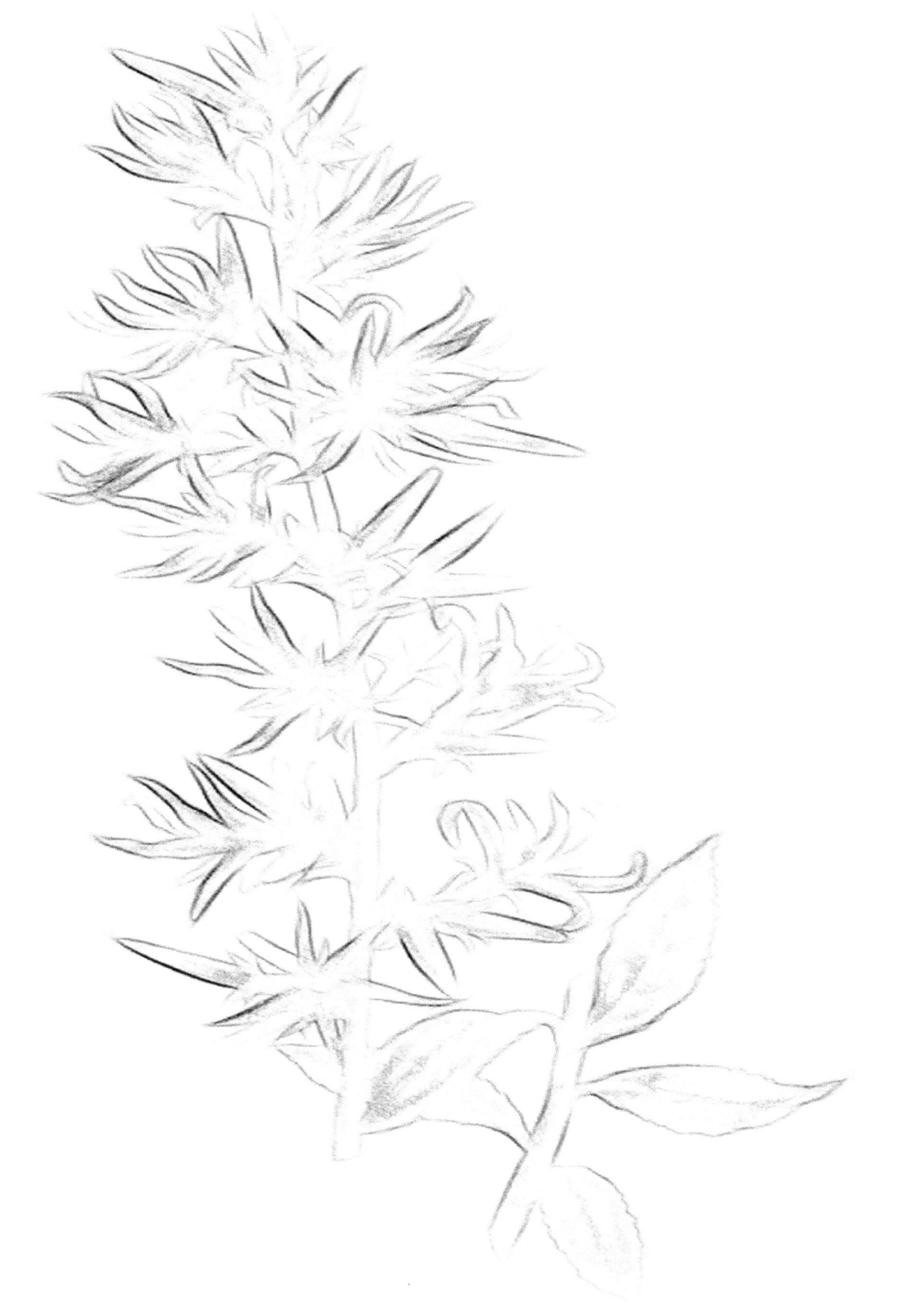

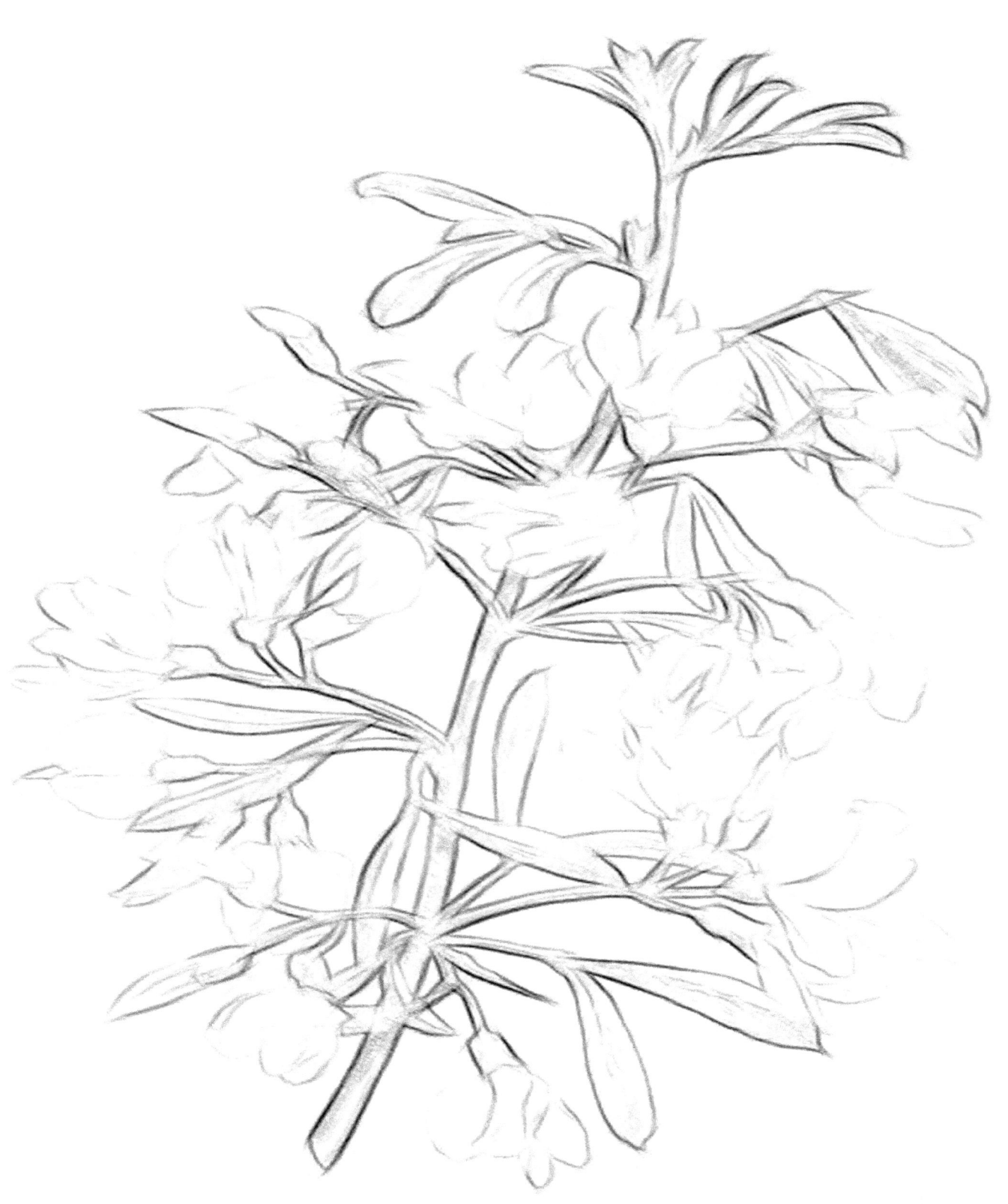

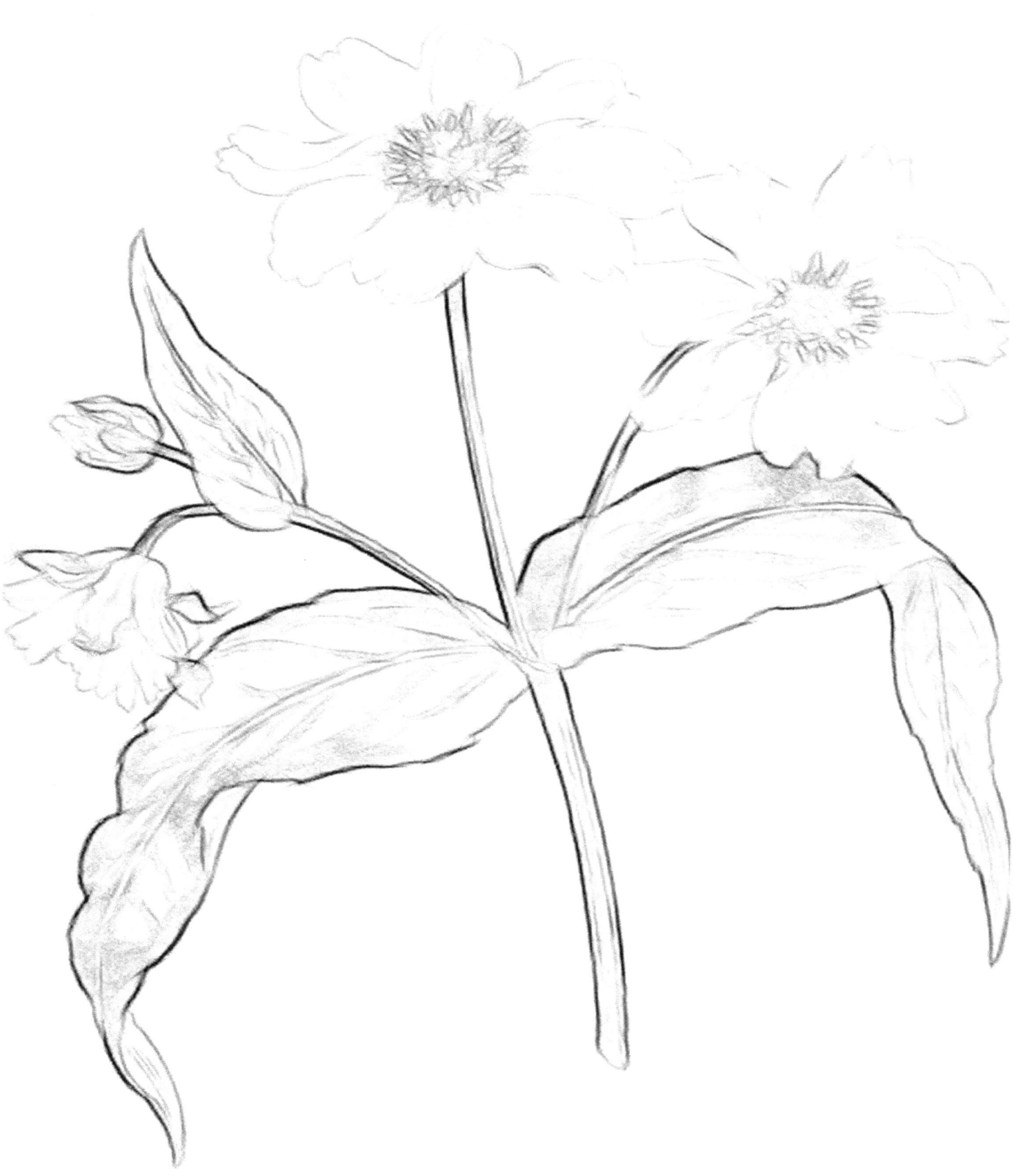

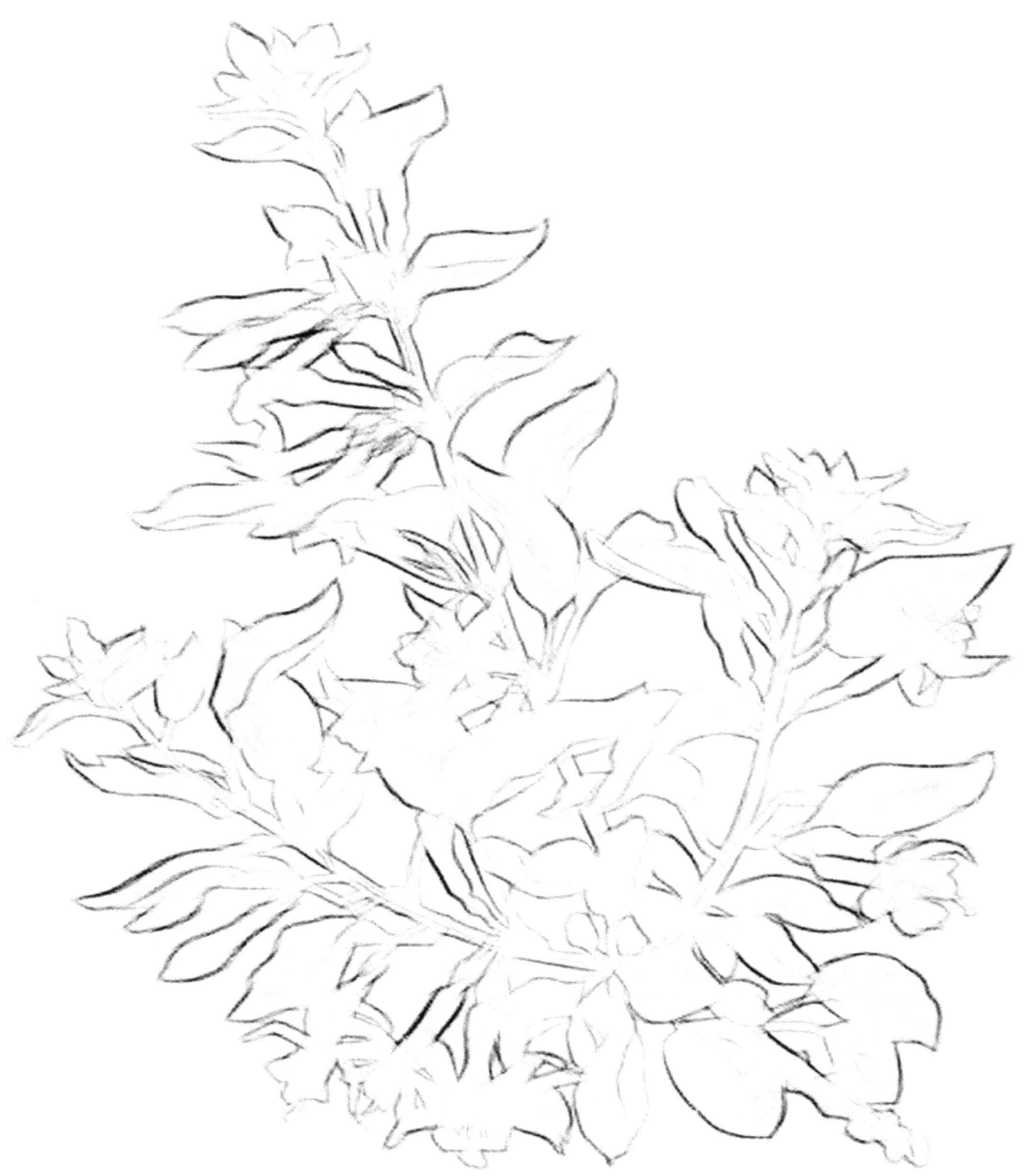

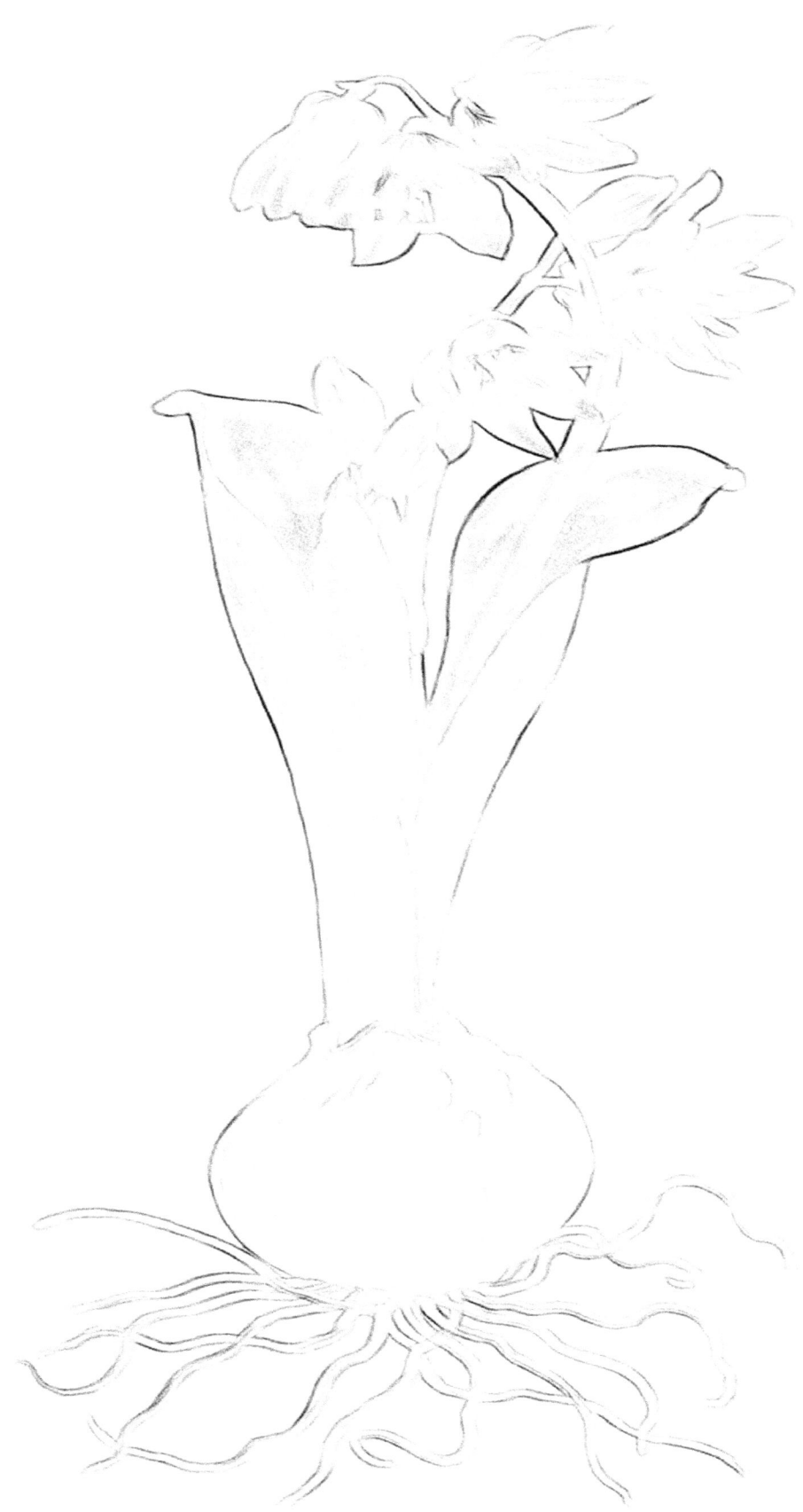

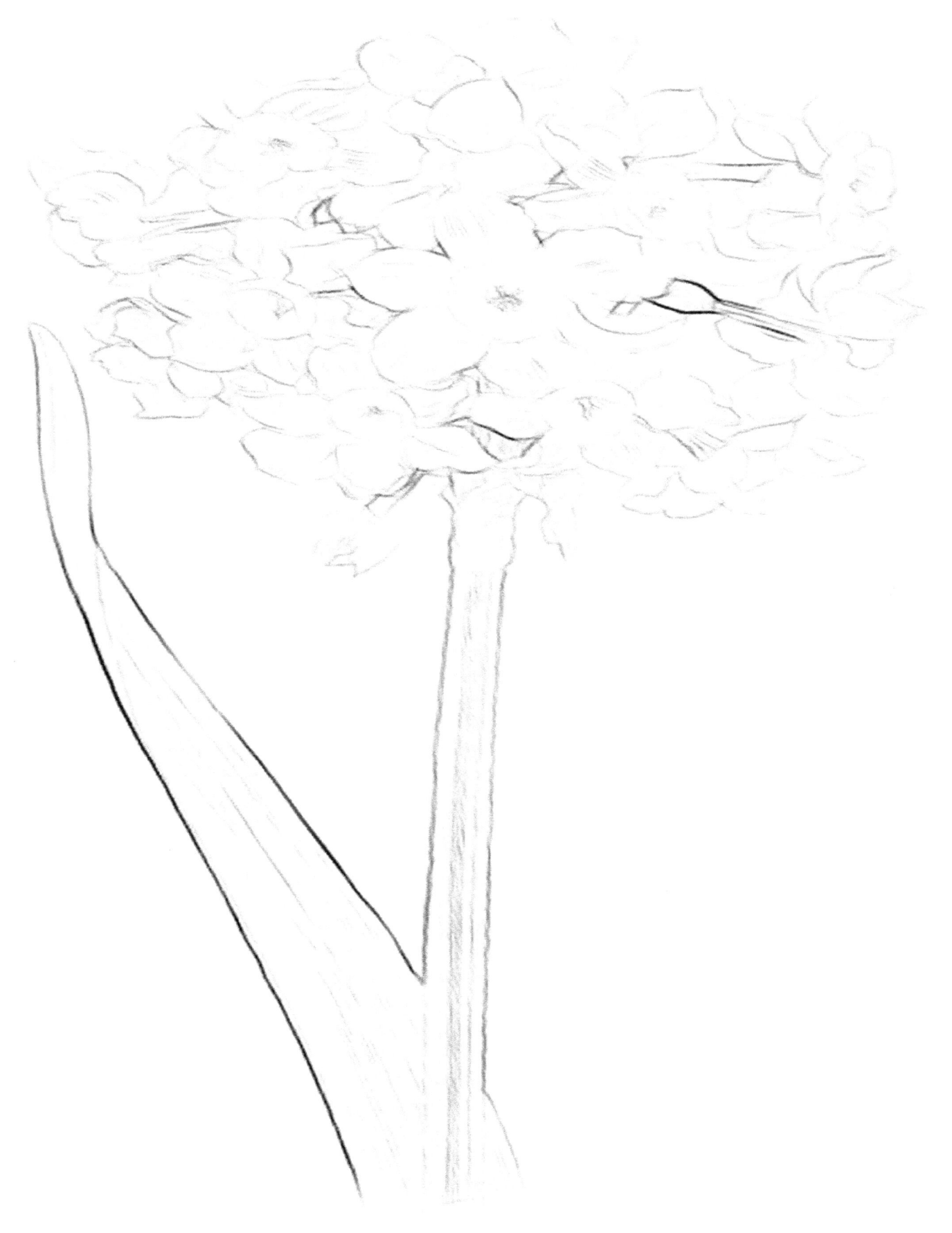